Christology
of the
Armenian Church

Rev. Dr. Vrej Nersessian

ISBN: 1492242071
ISBN-13: 978-1492242079

Editor & Publisher
Edgar Ter-Danielyan

London

2013

DEDICATION

To my teachers and mentors: Archbishop Tiran Nersoyan,
Profs. C.E. Gunton, C.F. Evans, Graham N. Stanton, M. Nicol,
E.L. Mascall, Maurice Frank Wiles, Philip Owen Sherrard.

« Որդյ յիշատակն օրՀնութեամբ եղիցի, Ա՛մէն »

ACKNOWLEDGMENTS

I wish to express my sincere thanks to my friend Edgar Ter-Danielyan for the support he has given to reading and preparing this manuscript for printing.

i

HISTORICAL BACKGROUND

The main line of advance of Christianity into Armenia was from the important base of Caesarea in Cappadocia, the neighbouring country to the west of Armenia. According to the 6th century canon of the Council of Nicaea the exarch of Caesaria had supervisory jurisdiction for the missionary districts to the east of the exarchate. Consequently for about sixty years after the consecration of Saint Gregory the Illuminator as Catholicos of Armenia, his successors were ordained by the exarchs of Caesaria. After the year 373 open canonical ties with Caesaria were severed - the church had become sufficiently strong and mature, its clergy had increased in numbers and its authority had been firmly established. However, because of this historical association the orientation of the Armenian Church in the matter of doctrine was always determined by the Alexandrian school of thought.

In this the Council of Ephesus (431), the council at which the Alexandrian position became victorious, was the dominant factor. The first patristic works translated into Armenian were the writings of St. Basil, Gregory the Thaumaturgas, Gregory Nazianzus, Gregory of Nyssa, John Chrysostom, Ephraem the Syrian, Athanasius of Alexandria, Cyril of Alexandria and few others. These writings were predominantly Alexandrian in their approach to the Christological questions of the time. Thus the Alexandrian atmosphere that existed in the first half of the fifth century was decisive in deciding the orientation of the Armenian Church.

CHURCH COUNCILS

The Armenian Church, together with the other Oriental Orthodox churches, recognizes the doctrinal and canonical validity of the first three councils of the Christian church - namely the Council of Nicaea (325), the Council of Constantinople (381) and the Council of Ephesus (431). She reveres them as holy, and has special days in the liturgical year dedicated to each one of them, celebrated with special hymns and ceremonies. As a fifth century church father puts it, the Armenian Church regards the doctrinal decisions of these councils as "*The basis of life and guide to the path leading to God*". She has given them authority by which all statements concerning the Christian faith are judged. By them certain statements are reckoned and rejected as additions to the Tradition of the divine revelation. This attitude is best expressed by a doctrinal statement recited in the Divine Liturgy of the Armenian Church just after recitation of the Nicaean Creed:

As for those who say there was a time when the Son was not or there was a time when the Holy Spirit was not or that they came into being out of nothing or who say that the Son of God or the Holy Spirit are of different substance and that they are changeable or alterable, such the catholic and apostolic holy church doth anathematize.

This statement added to the Creed refutes Arianism, Macedonianism, Apollinarianism and Nestorianism. Instead the Armenian Church confesses and proclaims:

As for us, we shall glorify him who was before the ages, worshipping the Holy Trinity and the one Godhead, the Father and the Son and the Holy Spirit, now and always and unto the ages of ages.

In order to understand and appreciate the dogmatic position of the Armenian Church on the later developments of the Christological issues, it is necessary to briefly review the situation in the church in the fifth century.

"FOR US AND FOR OUR SALVATION"

The church as a whole has always believed that it is important to maintain the doctrine that Christ is both God and man. If we say that Christ is God and not man, then all that was human in the historical Jesus disappears, including his ability to suffer and to feel as we feel. In fact, Jesus ceases to be our Example, because what was possible for him as God is not necessarily possible for us as men. There are also difficulties if we say that Christ is man and not God, to put it mildly. If Jesus were only a man, just as other men are, our doctrine of God and redemption would be impoverished to such a degree that it would be unattainable. Christians maintain the central teaching, that God was so good, so interested in the affairs of men, that he himself devised a means of our salvation, and "sent" Jesus for our redemption. Thus, the denial of either the divinity or the manhood of Christ implies consequences disastrous to the Christian conception of God. Christianity is the only fully historical religion. It is the only religion that actually depends entirely upon history. It is faith in the Incarnate God, it is Divine redemption given from within history, not by the promulgation of doctrines but by the wrenching of one Man's flesh and the spilling of his blood upon one particular square yard of ground, outside one particular city gate during three particular unrepeatable hours, which could have been measured on a clock.

ALEXANDRIA AND ANTIOCH

Though the Church as a whole has always recognised the importance of retaining the full belief in both the divinity and the manhood of Christ, there have generally been two schools of thought within her fold, one of which lays stress on the divinity, and the other which places emphasis upon the manhood of Christ. In the ancient church these two rival tendencies were displayed respectively by the theological schools of Alexandria and Antioch.

The Antiochene school was, on the whole, more concerned with the life and human experience of Christ and sought to make a clear distinction between the human and the divine natures. Diodorus of Tarsus, one of the leading theologians of this school, distinguished in Christ, the Son of God from the Son of David, in whom the Word dwelt "as in a temple". He considered that the man born of Mary was the Son of God not by nature but by the grace, only the Word being the Son of God by nature. The stress on the distinction between the two natures rather than on their union, was more marked in the teaching of Theodore of Mopsuestia, who looked upon the union as a conjunction of distinct elements, and stated that "not God, but the temple in which God dwelt is born of the Virgin Mary". This separation was even carried further by Nestorius, Patriarch of Constantinople. The latter claimed that the two natures had remained complete and distinct after the union, each one retaining its specific properties and acting according to them.

The union in Christ was, according to Nestorius, a personal union. This conception led to the recognition of two Sons in Jesus Christ, for the person of Jesus Christ resulting from the Incarnation was not absolutely identical with that of the Word, before the Incarnation. This doctrine, in the final analysis, threatened the doctrine of Redemption since salvation could not have been achieved by a man; humanity could not have been saved if God himself had not suffered and died on the cross.

Alexandrian theology started from the concept of the divinity of Christ. Its exponents insisted more on the divinity of the Word Incarnate and the intimate and complete union of the two natures in the person of Christ. St. Cyril of Alexandria taught that the person of Christ is identical with that of the Word; the Word incarnate is Jesus Christ and is complete in his divinity. But the humanity that the Word has assumed, and in which He lives, is also complete, being composed of a body animated by a rational soul. "The two distinct natures," he wrote, "had united into a true union, and from both one Christ and one Son had come, not as though the difference of the natures had been done away by the union, but, on the contrary, that they constituted the one Lord Jesus Christ and Son by the unutterable union of the Godhead and the manhood." Saint Cyril defined this intimate union by the formula "*One incarnate nature of God the Word*". There is one Son in Jesus Christ and He, being identical with the Word, is the Son of God; this same Word incarnate is the Son of Mary by nature, and thus Mary is "Godbearer" (*Theotokos*) and not just the "bearer of Christ" (*Christotokos*), a term preferred by the Antiochene school.

The Christology of Saint Cyril triumphed at the Council of Ephesus in 431, and Nestorius and his supporters were condemned as heretics. But this teaching was gradually deformed by some of his followers, especially by Eutyches, the archimandrite of a monastery in Constantinople. Eutyches so emphasised the union that the two natures in Christ were confused and the manhood seemed to be absorbed by the Godhead. He denied that the *body* of the Saviour was of the same substance as ours, and this naturally raised the question whether the manhood of Christ was true manhood or merely docetic.

COUNCIL OF CHALCEDON

The Tome of Leo represents the opposite view to the concept just outlined. Leo I and the Council of Chalcedon suspected Eutyches of teaching a form of Docetism, that is, the denial of Christ's truly human nature, and, thus, of incarnation as such. Therefore Leo emphasised the difference of divinity and humanity in Christ in the Roman tradition. The most important expressions in the Chalcedonian formulation were to be the following:

Each nature performs what is proper to itself in common with the other; the Word, that is, performing what is proper to the Word, and the flesh carrying out what is proper to the flesh, the one shines out in miracles, the other succumbs to injuries.

Although there is in the Person of the Lord Jesus one Person of God and man, yet that wherein the suffering is common to both is one thing, and that wherein the glory is common is another, for from us He has the humanity inferior to the Father, and from the Father He has divinity equal to the Father.

In order to pay the debt of our condition, the invisible Nature was united to a passible, so that, as was necessary for our healing, one and the same Mediator between God and man, the Man Jesus Christ, should be able from one to die and from the other should not be able to die.

Contrary to the Cyrilline-Alexandrian concept, Leo made the flesh, that is,

Christ's human nature, into a centre of autonomous activity. All these ideas had, in fact, been conserved by both the Alexandrine and Antiochene traditions in the East. The clash between them was the result of fear on the part of the former that the latter was not affirming the unity of Christ's Person in any real sense. The Tome appeared to be expounding the doctrine of the two natures to the entire satisfaction of the Antiochene side.

CHALCEDON AND THE ARMENIAN CHURCH

The Armenian Church having come under the influence of Alexandrian Christological teaching on purely theological grounds, from the middle of the fourth century, repudiated the new doctrinal formulations of the Council of Chalcedon. The Chalcedonian Definition drafted in the same council was judged to be deviating from the line of thought drawn up by St. Cyril and sanctioned by the Council of Ephesus. The Armenian Church did not react against the Council of Chalcedon only upon the instigation and influence of the Syrian Church nor were they misled because of the deficiency of their language in its capacity to render correctly the subtleties of the Greek expressions. Neither did they exploit the doctrinal issues for purely political and nationalistic purposes. The theological discussions were based on the Greek terms and conceptions and all the leaders of the Armenian Church in those centuries knew Greek as well as anybody else.

In spite of the political unrest in Armenia at the time of the council (the momentous Battle of Avarayr for the defence of the faith against Persians was fought in the same year 451) the Armenian Church had soon the knowledge of the decisions of the council and was able to fully participate in the discussions that followed. After long debates they deeply resented the new formulations, which were regarded as alien to the traditional Christology of the time and revealed close association with the dyophysite Christology already condemned in the teaching of Nestorius. The action of the Armenian Church and other "Pre-Chalcedonian" churches was simply to vindicate the position they had already taken all along together with the rest of the church, as early as the fifth century.

"MONOPHYSITISM"

In examining the reasons why the Armenian Church and the other non-Chalcedonian churches adopted the stand they took against the formulations of the Tome of Leo and the Definition of the Council of Chalcedon it is necessary to see whether they criticised the council from a monophysite point of view, an accusation sometimes attributed to them by the Chalcedonian churches.

The question, "What is monophysitism?" therefore needs a few words of clarification. A compound of the Greek words, *monos* and *physis* used adjectively in English, the term monophysite means "one-natured" or "single-natured". It is explained by Walter F. Adeney in these words: "*The Monophysites*", he writes, "*had contended that there was only one nature in Christ, the human and the divine being fused together, because the two did not meet on equal terms, and the overwhelming of the Finite left for our contemplation only the Infinite*".

The Oxford Dictionary of the Christian Church (3rd ed., 2003) describes Monophysitism as "*The doctrine that in the Person of the Incarnate Christ there is only one nature, not two … covers a variety of positions, some capable of orthodox interpretation, others not.*" Thus by this definition, ideas that were ascribed to Eutyches were also ascribed to the non-Chalcedonian churches. Broadly speaking, these accusations may be classified under three headings:

- a tendency to ignore the manhood of Christ,
- a teaching which ignores Human properties in Jesus Christ and
- a teaching which maintains that the Manhood of Christ was Incorruptible.

One of the bases on which the term Monophysitism is used with reference to the non-Chalcedonian churches is its defence of the use of the phrase "One incarnate nature of God the Word". There are three emphases made by this phrase "One incarnate nature":

- it was God the Son Himself who became incarnate,
- in becoming incarnate, He individuated manhood in union with Himself and made it His very own,
- the incarnate Word is one Person.

The "One" in the phrase "One incarnate nature" is not a simple one, so that the characterization "monophysite" cannot be considered applicable to the position held by the Armenian Church. In the Incarnation, by a divine act of condescension, God the Son willed to be so united with manhood that the two of them came together, without either of them being lost or diminished. At the same time, their union was so real and perfect that Christ was "one incarnate nature".

DOCTRINE OF THE ARMENIAN CHURCH

In face of the misunderstanding expressed by the Chalcedonian tradition described above, we shall put together the ideas emphasized by some of the Armenian theologians on those specific points of doctrine. According to the Armenian Apostolic Church the Orthodox faith is that Our Lord is perfect in His Godhead and perfect in His Manhood. They dare not say, however, that He is God and Man together, for this expression implies separation. He is rather God Incarnate. In Him the Godhead and the Manhood are united in a complete union: that is to say in essence, hypostasis and nature. There is no separation between the Godhead and the Manhood of Our Lord. From the very moment of the descent of the Divine Word, in the Virgin's womb, the Second Person of the Trinity took to Himself, from Mary's blood, a human body with a rational soul, and made Himself one with the manhood, which He received from the Holy Virgin. Mary's child is God Incarnate, one essence, one person, one hypostasis, one nature: one nature out of two natures. In the *Teaching of Saint Gregory* the doctrine of the Incarnation is expounded in the following terms:

God the Holy Son was sent from God (The Father); he took flesh from the Virgin (and became) perfect man with perfect Godhead; he showed forth the power of the divinity and exposed the weakness of the flesh; those who believed in the flesh (he) manifested to them his Godhead; and those who erred (in their belief concerning) the flesh they denied his nature (i.e. his human nature). He united (himself) to the flesh in (his) nature and mixed the flesh with his Godhead; ... the true faith is this: He descended and mixed (his) Godhead with (our) manhood and the immortal with the mortal so that he could make us participants in the immortality of his Godhead; thus, when the Son of God equal to the Father, came with his flesh to the right of his Father, he united us to God.

Hence the union in which the Armenian Church believes in differs essentially and substantially from the kind of union professed by Eutyches. Eutyches maintained that our Lord is one nature, but that the manhood of Christ is absorbed in His divinity and completely vanishes like a drop of vinegar in the sea. In fact he is denying the real existence of the manhood of Christ. The Armenian Apostolic Church takes an opposite position in professing that Christ is One nature, completely preserved in which are all the human properties as well as all the divine properties, without confusion, mixture or alteration. Several doctrinal documents belonging to various periods, make clear how the Armenian Church understood the union of the two natures.

The first of these documents is a treatise ascribed to the famous Armenian historian of the fifth century Moses Khorenatsi. Speaking against those who

9

separate Christ in two, he asserts very strongly the idea of unity right from the very beginning by saying that it is possible for many elements to join together and to be united in one nature. Man is composed of earthly and spiritual elements, but he has one nature. The two are not confused in him, that is to say, the flesh is not soul and the soul is not flesh. Each maintains its own properties. Their union does not destroy the distinctness of the two. Likewise the Incarnation also must be understood in the same manner. We must confess Christ One in His nature because it is said "the Word became flesh" and that "He took the form of a servant". The meaning of the Scriptures is clear: that which was taken by the Word was that which he did not have. Therefore, the two, the Word and the flesh, which were separate before the Incarnation, became One after the Incarnation.

Half a century later, when the controversy over the use of the term "natures" was more acute, the Armenian theologian Yovhannes Mandakuni composed his *Demonstration* in which he analyzed the meaning of this word and the legitimacy of its application to Christ. This work is one of the most sober and erudite of the many studies composed in Armenian in defence of their position. Yovhannes acknowledges that the term "nature" has different connotations. One can speak of the natures of the body, of the soul, and of the mind, and these are all different; yet man is not many, but one. Similarly, the many names of Christ do not involve several persons or natures, but only one Lord. Christian tradition, summed up at Nicaea, speaks of the single nature of the Son who is of the essence of his Father, so John can say that the Son is of the same nature as the Father. Hence the name of the Son is his divinity. But this term is not scriptural, so Yovhannes suggests that "life" would be more appropriate to indicate the single personality of Christ. Yovhannes thus realises that "nature" does not necessarily mean "person", but the traditional identification of these two terms is still influential enough to lead him to stress that the acts of Christ can be ascribed to only one nature, for the Lord is one.

The Incarnation is thus to be conceived as the indivisible union of the Logos and the flesh, but the subject of discourse is always the divine Word. The Logos was incarnate, became a man, and was united to the flesh, and this flesh is said to be the flesh of the Word by a true union. But the Word did not become flesh by nature, for then the flesh would be the Word, which is ridiculous. So Christ was by will and not by nature in the flesh; He is God with the flesh, and with this same body (for Armenian does not distinguish "flesh" and "body") He will come again. Thus there are two points that he refutes categorically at the outset. The first is the idea of union as understood by those who in fact separate Christ in two. For him the union is genuinely real one and not a sheer principle of union or indwelling of the Word in the flesh. *"Some consider that the descending (the Incarnation) was in appearance and not in truth. They believe that Christ became man in the sense that He inhabited the flesh by complaisance and will"*. Here, in fact, he is criticising the ideas propounded in the name of Theodore of Mopsuestia who was influential in the bordering countries of Armenia. Secondly, he criticises the Chalcedonian position for its dualistic interpretation of Christ's life and death. The distinctness of the two natures has led the dyophysite thinkers so far as to give each nature the meaning of a person. It is this hypostasized understanding of Christ's natures, as the Tome of Leo formulates so sharply, that was fiercely opposed by the Armenian Church together with the other non-Chalcedonian churches. The core of the position of the Armenian Church can be found in the following passage of the *Demonstration* of Yovhannes Mandakuni:

God the Word took flesh and became man; thus, He united to Himself in God-fitting manner, the body of our lowliness, the whole soul and flesh; and the flesh truly became the flesh of the Word of God. In virtue of this it is said of the Invisible that He is seen, of the Intangible that He is felt, crucified, buried and risen on the third day. For He Himself was both the passible, and the impassible, the immortal who received death.

It is clear from these documents, that the Armenian doctrine of the nature of Christ firmly asserts the oneness of the two natures of Christ, and not a unification of the two natures. One nature out of two natures unconfused and indivisible without change or diminution. If we designate separately Christ's manhood and His divine manifestation there would be no reason, as Timothy Aelurus denotes, not to distinguish in Him, say seven natures, such as chemical, the vegetal, the animal, the rational, the angelic and the divine; the latter being the most comprehensive one dominating the other natures. We stress that the divine and the human natures were indivisible, united in Christ; so united that though we distinguish the two yet they are not distinctly different, but unity in One person. Therefore we can no longer say that each stands separate in itself and performs deeds at its discretion, but we believe that the thought of one necessarily gives rise to the thought of the other.

The attempt of the Chalcedonians to conceive the one apart from the other would be as perverse as for any one to represent the human body as a man in and by itself. It is improper to designate Christ as a man who became God, but only as God who became man; not a *conversion* into flesh and bones, but *assumption* of flesh and bones. When the evangelist says *"the Word became flesh"*, he refers to the divine as sharing in all that Christ experienced as man. The dogmatic statements contained in the writings of Armenian theologians are directed towards the retention of a principle of unity, while at the same time they concede the diversity of the predicates, and aim to characterise all the deeds and sufferings of Christ as at once divine and human. The conception of the Tome of Leo and the Chalcedonian formulations, as it was seen does the contrary, for they allot one function to the divine, and another to the human nature, even after the union. God and man were indeed, in Christ, one person, one Unity.

NERSES SHNORHALI'S DEFINITION OF FAITH

St Nerses IV Klayetsi, Catholicos of All Armenians, better known by the epithet Shnorhali (full of grace), 1102-73, Armenian churchman, theologian, diplomat, poet and musician, was the greatest literary figure of the Silver Age of the 12th century.

Shnorhali, whose epithet was given to brilliant students of the monastery school of the Karmir Vank (Red Monastery), was born in the fortress of Dzovk to Prince Apirat Pahlavouni, and was the great-grandson of Grigor Magistros (990-1059). The fortress was situated in the province of Tlouk, part of the demesnes of Prince Vasil, Shnorhali's brother, which eventually became part of the Armenian Cilician Kingdom (1090- 1375). Nerses received his education at the monastic school, under the guidance of bishop Stepannos Manouk. He was ordained priest and then bishop by his elder brother Grigor III Pahlavouni (1093-1166).

In 1141 he with his brother, Catholicos Gregory, participated in the Church Council held in Antioch, the first official contact between the Latin and Armenian Churches. In April 1166 Catholicos Grigor Pahlavouni appointed Nerses coadjutor catholicos and he conducted the administrative duties of the See until his death. Shnorhali's literary career extended over half a century. The relative security of the Cilician Armenian Kingdom gave new impetus to Armenian cultural activities and ushered in the so-called Silver Age. He wrote poems, commentaries, anthems, hymns, theological treatises and encyclicals.

One of the most remarkable aspects of Nerses Shnorhali's career was his unremitting endeavour to recover the unity of the Armenian and Byzantine Churches. He issued four Encyclicals on church unity: three of them (1166, 1170, and 1173) were addressed to Emperor Manuel I Comnenus (1143-80), and the fourth to Patriarch Michael III (1170-8). Nerses IV Klayetsi was the ecumenical figure par excellence of the Christian church. His continuous negotiations with the Byzantine Emperor, for the reunion of the Armenian and Greek Churches, constitutes one of the brightest chapters in the history of ecumenical   discussion. He produced doctrinal treatises to prove the Orthodoxy of the Armenian Church: *The Confession of Faith of the Armenian Church* and *Definition of Faith of the Armenian Church*. What is notable about his approach is that, in contrast to the maximalist attitude of the Greeks, who tended to demand that the Armenian Church conform in all ritual and ceremonial usage as well as in all dogmatic formulae to their traditions, Nerses insists that complete uniformity is necessary only in the most basic doctrinal essentials; to demand more, he says, is to risk falling into the Pharisaic legalism condemned by Jesus as elevating human traditions above the Word of God.

DEFINITION OF FAITH
OF THE ARMENIAN CHURCH

Written By Nerses Catholicos of All Armenians At The Request of Emperor Manuel The God-Loving King of The Greeks

"As we have learnt from the Holy Fathers, we confess the property of the distinctiveness of the Father as being unborn and without beginning, and the birth of the Son of the Father who is without beginning, uncreated and timeless, and the procession, and emanation and the sending forth of the Spirit from the Father ineffably.

The Father is said to be Father for having been the cause of the birth of the Son and of the procession of the Spirit. And the Son is said to be Son not because of a corruptible birth after physical beings, as some blind-minded people think, but because He is of the nature of the Father and is not a creature, and the manner of His birth is incomprehensible to creatures. He is also called Only-Begotten, because there is no one either before or after Him born of the Father. He is also said to be the Logos (Word), because His birth is without corruption, just as our speech is born of mind.

Nor is the Father first and then the Son, as is the law of our fluid and generative nature, but, as the Father is eternal, so eternal also is the Son, together with the eternal Father, and everlastingly with Him in the beginning and in the end, resembling the rays originating from the sun. As neither the sun nor the light is first, but both appear simultaneously, similarly the Son as light is born of the Father, who is light, and He is everlastingly with Him. And as there is no sun without its light, and no image without its prototype, so also neither is there a Father without a Son, nor a Son without Father, for He is the light of glory and the image of His essence, for the Father is glory, and the Son is the light of the glory; the Father is the original and the Son is the image of the invisible God the

Father; for that reason we believe the Son to be consubstantial and co-creator with the Father.

We also confess the Holy Spirit as truly the Spirit of God and it is not due to the homonymity that we compare Him with the creaturely spirits, as we do not equate the only Son by nature with those who are sons of God by grace; for, by being called the Spirit of God, He differs from the spirits that are made.

Having come forth from the Father in-originate as a person who is perfect and without beginning, He is incomprehensible and ineffable to us who are creatures; according to the essence of the cause He is from the only Father, but He possesses and distributes gifts equally with the Father and the Son, as the Son says of the same Holy Spirit: "He does not speak of Himself, but He receives from me and tells, for, He says, everything that the Father has is mine". He has no beginning in time and suffers no change like created beings. He is the one who searches the unsearchable depths of God and reveals His unrevealed mysteries. He is of the same essence with the Father and the Son, with respect to everlastingness, and shares their glory and creativity, having the same power and honour.

We also confess these three persons having come together being united in one Godhead and not separated from one another by different natures, introducing any time period or creature between them (as per Arius), but we believe and recognize one nature of the Most Holy Trinity, one dominion, one power, one glory. And again, we do not join Sabellius of Libya, who follows the Jewish teaching that the three persons are gathered in one, but we separate them inseparably and we unify them distinctly according to the doctrine of the orthodox Fathers.

For we believe in three persons, neither more nor less than three, and one nature, not divided into three according to personalities, but as the Church recognized from the glorification of the seraphim, in the threefold Sanctus, by bringing together dominion and Godhead. Nor are they distinguished one from the other by nature as Adam, Seth and Eve are not distinguished even though one is unbegotten and the other is begotten, and the other is unbegotten, being born of Adam. Even so, the Father being unbegotten and the Son being begotten and the Holy Spirit proceeding from the Father, they are not thereby separated according to nature.

None of the three of equal honour is greater by nature than the others with whom He has been associated, for though the Father was said to be great, He is great for being the cause and not because of His nature, since by nature He is co-equal with the Son and the Spirit.

The divinity of the Father was not less before nor gradually in the course of time completed, or as if there was a time when the Father was not because of His not having the Son, or as if He was not wise because of His not carrying the wisdom in His bosom, and not powerful because of the power not being with Him, for according to the Apostle, Christ is the power of God and the wisdom of God; nor not reasonable, because of the Reason (Word) not being with God from the beginning, according to John; or as if He did not have life because there was a time when the life giving Spirit was not with Him.

But the Father is always Father by having in Him immutably the Word, the power and the wisdom and the life; and the Son is eternally Son born of the Father and being always with the Father, and the Holy Spirit is everlastingly the Spirit of God and with God. The Father is Himself cause and the Son and the Spirit are from the cause without time and without cause. The Father has His origin from no one and the Son and the Spirit have their origin from the Father. But the Son and the Spirit being before time and nature are co-creators with the Father.

Time and those that are subject to time, namely, intelligent and sensible creatures, have been brought into being out of nothing. We confess that one of the three persons, the Son, who by the will of the Father and the Spirit, and by the annunciation of the archangel Gabriel came down to earth, which He has made and where He always was and which He provided for. While He remained undiminished and undescended the incomprehensible one of the creatures was contained in the womb of the Virgin from whom He assumed our sinful and corruptible nature, soul and mind and body, He mixed and united it with His sinless and incorruptible nature and by them He became one and indivisible, thereby changing not the nature of His body into incorporeity, but the sinful flesh into sinless flesh and the corruptible into incorruptible and the mortal into immortal. When He willed keeping His divine and human essence unchanged in the union, He was conceived and after a period of nine months He was born of the Virgin, the virginity of the bearer remaining intact. And the One who was born of the Father incorporeally, was born of the mother corporeally, and the Son of God became son of man, not one becoming Son of God and one Son of Man, and not dividing the one Son into two sons, according to the blasphemy of Nestorius.

For the Logos did not dwell in body, but was encased into a body not by change, but by unification. He did not encase His body in the virgin's womb by a creative act, as some of the heretics say, but He assumed body from the virgin, which was not alien to her nature, but of the same. And not in apparent, as if passing through a tube, according to Eutyches and those who thought like him, but He truly put on real body of the constitution of Adam, with a new mixing and a wondrous mixture, being above and beyond to all simile.

For from the beginning there was no mixture and union between the Creator and a creature; the union of God with man is compared to the co-mixture of soul and body to a limited extent and not in every way, as Gregory of Nyssa in his book on Nature under the chapter on the Unity of the Soul and Body, says: "Porphyry, who uses his tongue against Christ, testifies to these, because the testimonies of the enemies in our favour are stronger and do not need contradiction". This Porphyry, he says, is writing thus in his second discourse: "It cannot be said that it is impossible that one essence be the complementary of another essence, to be with another and while keeping its own essence intact not changing its own superiority, but changing it by proximity to its energy". He says this of the union of the soul and body. And if these words on the soul concerning incorporeity are true, then how much more is it true of the Word of God, which is ever beyond comparison and truly incorporeal.

And we agree with these and believe that according to John, the Word became flesh; He did not change into flesh by losing His nature, but by joining the flesh, He truly became flesh and remained without flesh, as He was from the beginning: it is not that one is flesh and the other without flesh, but that the same Christ is both flesh and without flesh, flesh by virtue of the human nature which He assumed, and without flesh by virtue of the divine nature which He had. And the same is visible and invisible, tangible and intangible, in time and without time, Son of Man and Son of God, consubstantial with the Father by virtue of the Godhead, and consubstantial with us by virtue of the manhood. Neither one nor both of these, but one essence and one personality out of two natures united in one Christ without confusion and without division in unity. Although the human mind fails in these things as they are above nature, nothing is impossible for the divine power; for, if soul and body, having been created by God, can be one nature out of two opposites and neither loses its essence in the union, then how much more the all-powerful nature of God has the capability and possibility of becoming flesh while remaining without flesh, to get mixed with the nature of the created man and yet to keep the uncreated nature, which is of the Father, unchanged?

And as we confess Him to have been one out of two natures and not having lost one of the two in the union, in the same way we do not say of the will as being one and other, as if the divine will were opposed to the human will, or the human to the divine; but we say that out of one essence, the wills being dual according to the difference of time, sometimes divine when He willed to manifest the power of His Godhead, and sometimes human when He willed to reveal the humility of His manhood. And these are the manifestations not of opposition, but of free will, because it was not the human will that forced itself upon the divine, as it is in us, when the will of the flesh desires in opposition to the soul, but the human followed the divine will, for when He willed and permitted, then the body would be given to its own desires, as at the temptation, when after the completion of the forty-day fast, when He willed to permit the nature of the body to hunger. For though He said that the Father's will was different from His, according to what is said "not as I will, but as thou wilt", this is a manifestation of the accord of the Son with the will of the Father and not of opposition. This is explained elsewhere as being something proper to the divinity and not to the incarnate body: "I descended from heaven not to do my own will, but my Father's will", and it is evident that what descended from heaven was the incorporeal Godhead and not body, which He took after descending on the earth.

And concerning the Godhead how would one dare to separate the Son's will from that of the Father, and what the Father's will is the Son shows by saying, "This is the will of my Father, that I will give eternal life to all those who believe in me"? Now, it is the Father"s will to give life to those who believe in the Son; and does not the Son have His will? Especially by these words the Son shows His accord with the will of the Father and not His opposition, after Gregory the Theologian.

For, states Gregory, when the Son says to the Father, "Not my will, but thine be done which is also mine", He shows that His will and the Father's will are one. Because if all that is of the Father is also of the Son, and whatever is of the Son is of the Father, it is clear then that the Father's will is also the will of the Son and the Son's will is the Father's will.

On the example of the will of which we spoke showing that out of one free will of the Godhead, there are two wills, the divine and the human, that are unopposed so also we believe that in the union similarly the operation is divine and human. And we do not attribute the highest things to the Godhead only, apart from the flesh, and not the lowest things to the manhood alone, apart from the divine. For if it were not so, how could it be said that the Son of Man came down from heaven or that God was crucified, His blood being that of God? We therefore confess both these to belong to the one person of the Son, sometimes as God operating the things divine as God, and sometimes the things human as man. Thus His works of dispensation also manifest from the beginning to the end.

For although He was conceived as man, yet as God He was conceived by the Holy Spirit. He was born of a woman as man, yet of a virgin, and He kept the virginity of the bearer immaculate after His birth as God. When eight days old He was circumcised as man, and He removed the circumcision of the body, being the giver of the law of circumcision, He taught the circumcision of the heart. He was presented in the Temple as man when forty days old, yet He was testified by Simeon as being God who releases the captives. He escaped Herod yet as man and as God He put idols to flight from Egypt. He was baptized by John as man, but washed off Adam's sin by His baptism, and He was testified by the Father and the Spirit as God. The new Adam was tempted like the old one, and as the Creator of Adam He defeated the tempter and as God He gave authority to the children of Adam to trample down the power of the enemy. He hungered as man, and as God He fed unopposed thousands with a few loaves. He thirsted as man, and as God He called to Him those who were thirsty in order to enable them to drink the water of life. He was tired on the road as man, but as God to the workers and to the heavily laden by sins He gave rest with His easy yoke and with His light burden. He slept in the boat as man, and as God He walked over the depths and He rebuked the wind and the sea. He paid tribute as man, but as God He created new coins from the mouth of the fish.

He prayed with us and for us as man, and as God together with His Father He accepted the prayers of all. He wept over His beloved as man, and as God He stopped the tears of the sisters by raising their brother. As man He asked "Where have you laid Lazarus?" and as God He raised by His voice him who had been dead for four days.

As man He was sold for a small price, and as God He purchased the world for a great price with His Blood. He became mute like a lamb before its slaughterer, according to His human nature, but by virtue of His divine nature He is the Word of God from the beginning, by which the heavens were established. He was nailed onto the wood with the robbers, as man, but as God He turned the daylight into darkness and He enabled the robber to enter paradise. He drank vinegar and He was fed with hyssop as man, but as God He changed the water into wine and became the sweetener of bitter foods. He died as man in His human nature and as God He raised the dead by divine power.

18

He tasted death in body inasmuch as He willed as man, and as God He destroyed death by death. Not one dead and one destroyer of death, but He himself dead and the same alive and giver of life to the dead, for He is one and the same Christ, as man being mortal by nature, but as God being immortal by nature.

The one united nature out of two was not divided into two, as if one was passible and dead and the other impassible and immortal, but the one united out of two opposites that has become one, bore the passions of each of the opposites, namely, the passions and death of the human nature, and the impassibility and immortality of the divine nature, because He, who died in body, the same was living by His divinity; He, who had suffered, the same was impassible, and He who sweated out of fear, was the same who pushed back those who came upon Him; and He who humbled Himself a little more than the angels, was strengthened by the angels and strengthens all the creatures; and He, who because of His divinity with the Father was the Creator of us, the creatures, the same was also creature because of His manhood with us, whom the preachers of the Word preach as perfect God and perfect Man, unified in a union higher than that of soul and body.

The human spirit being commended into the hands of the Father, was separated from the body, but the Godhead remained inseparable from both, for it was united with the rational soul, when it descended into hell to the souls it was inseparable from the dead body which was in the grave, not in part, but the whole Godhead being both with the body and the soul. Because the same was in the bosom of the Father and in the womb of the Virgin, in the seat of glory and in the manger, at the right hand of the Father and on the cross, among seraphim and in the grave, for heaven and earth are full of His glory; by rising on the third day, He became our resurrection and life; He ascended into heaven from where He never was absent. And He will come again to raise from the dead that are of Adam's nature and to judge the living and the dead in justice according to their faith and thoughts, words and deeds, by returning the good reward to those who are good, and returning to the wicked the verdict of the judgment of torment. And He will reign forever with those that were called to reign with Him in endless and everlasting ages. And then we shall know perfectly that knowledge of faith which we have now received only in measure, and which is in the Father and in the Son and in the Holy Spirit, and to whom glory and power unto the ages. Amen."

THEOTOKOS

The Armenian doctrine of the Virgin birth and redemption is also consistent with the above exposition of the doctrine of the nature of Christ. The Armenian Hymnal, which contains a rich collection of hymns dating from the fifth to the thirteenth centuries, renders the doctrine of the Incarnation from the realm of the mere speculation and lends to it the character of the pragmatic. Mary is the Bearer-of-God, a formula constantly reiterated to show that the Holy One who was born of her was God Himself made flesh. In one of the hymns sung during the feast of Christmas the Incarnation of Christ is described as:

Mystery Great and profound that has been revealed this day.
Shepherds sing with angels, giving good tidings to the earth
A new king is born in Bethlehem town.
Give blessings sons of men since for us he is incarnate.

The uncontainable in Earth and Heaven is
wrapped within swaddling clothes
From the Father inseparable, He seats Himself
in the Holy altar.

It follows from all this that the suffering of Christ is a Divine Sacrifice. Christ's death was a voluntary death, endured solely for our Salvation:

Thou Who in ineffable being
Art co-sharer of the Father's glory,
Didst voluntarily consent
To suffer in the flesh for us.

This last aspect of the doctrine of the nature of Christ involved the Armenian Church in the controversy concerning the corruptibility and incorruptibility of our Lord's body, a problem closely linked with the controversy of the nature of Christ. It would be only natural for the Armenian Church to affirm that our Lord's body was incorruptible. But this affirmation did not mean that Christ had a heavenly body in any sense or it was unreal because the Armenian Church has always confessed that Christ's body was passible.

The idea of the incorruptibility is that Christ being sinless, his body could not be affected by the consequences of sin. One of the arguments set forth in considering the Armenian doctrine Monophysite in the Eutychian sense is the form of the Trisagion as it is recited in the Armenian Liturgy: "*Holy*

God, Holy and powerful, Holy and immortal, who wast crucified for us". The controversial clause is *"Who wast crucified for us"*. This phrase is replaced by other appropriate phrases corresponding to the Dominical feast that is celebrated. For instance on Easter the wording is: *"Who didst rise from the dead"*; on Annunciation, Nativity, and Epiphany: *"Who wast born and manifested for us"*, and so forth. From this it is clear that the Trisagion is sung in honour of Christ, not of the Trinity, and inasmuch as the Godhead was present in Christ incarnate it was legitimate to say that God has been crucified for us, has risen from the dead and was born and manifested for us.

When we examine the non-Chalcedonian position carefully, we become convinced that the sole object of the reputed dissenters was to safeguard the divinely wrought redemption. It is their theology and soteriology, neither of them in question, that together determine their Christology. The Chalcedonians themselves although diophysites in their Christology, are forced into the miaphysite position when interpreting the saving work of our Lord. They feel that it is a suffering God, not man, that makes the Cross of Calvary significant. The letter of Pope Leo I to Flavian itself affirms as such. *"The impassible God,"* writes Leo, *"became a suffering man; the Immortal One submitted himself to the dominion of death."*

HERESIES REFUTED

The Armenian Church has always shunned Eutychianism and Severianism and all other teachings derived from this two lines of thought. Of the texts which prove the Armenian opposition to Eutychianism and Severianism, in addition to the passages already referred to, one need only mention here the treatise of the Catholicos Yovhannes Ojnetsi entitled *"Against the Phantasiasts"*.

In it the writer refutes with great vigour the erroneous beliefs of the latter, that the humanity of the Saviour was a mere modification, an external appearance like the imprint of the seal on a wax. He affirms that the Body of Christ is real and consubstantial with ours, and that the divine and human natures exist without confusion:

The Word, in becoming man and being called man, remained also God; and man, in becoming God and being called God, never lost his own substance. ... It is evident that it is the incomprehensible union and not the transformation of the natures which leads us to say one nature of the Word Incarnate. ... There is one nature and one person in Christ, if we must state it more briefly, and this is not because of the identity or the consubstantiality of the natures ... but, as I have frequently said, because of the ineffable union of the Word with His body.

To sum up the Armenian position, what they wished to say was that in the total being and action of Jesus Christ, both God and man are simultaneously and continually present and at work. The relationship between them is integral and persisting. To use here an excellent word, it is *unlooseable*. Once it has taken place, in accordance with the divine purpose, it is there; it cannot be undone. The objection to Chalcedon is not derived from a monophysite point of view; it came from a genuine fear that the council did not affirm the unity of Christ adequately, and that therefore it violated the faith of the Church. It is also clear that while opposing the council of Chalcedon and the Tome of Leo, the Armenian Church was fully aware of the Eutychian heresy, and that she excluded it with as much force and determination as the Chalcedonian side. Therefore, the reason for its opposition to Chalcedon was not an implicit or explicit sympathy for the position referred to as Eutychianism by the council of Chalcedon and the Tome of Leo.

The Armenian Church has its reasons for sticking to its traditional expression of the one nature that has the properties of the two natures without mixture, confusion or alteration. These reasons may be summed up as follows.

WITNESS OF THE SCRIPTURE

There is not a single Biblical text which proves decisively that Christ is two natures after the Union. Rather the reverse, all the Biblical texts are on the side of the Armenian position. Thus St. John is explicit: "The Word became flesh and dwelt among us". (1.4). In Revelation, Our Lord declares: "I am the first and the last, and the Living One, and I was dead, and behold I am alive for evermore and have the keys of Death and Hades" (1:17,18). The pronoun is "I" - there is no duality in this passage. It is He who is the first and the last, and it is He who was dead. The same meaning is clear in other passages: "And no man hath ascended into Heaven, but He that descended out of Heaven, even the Son of Man which is in Heaven" (John 3:13). In that case He is the One who is in Heaven, as well as being the Son of Man on earth. Aways the same one: one essence, one hypostasis, one nature. St. Paul, speaking to the Ephesian leaders, claims the same union: "Take heed unto yourselves and to all the flock in which the Holy Spirit hath made you bishops, to feed the Church of God which He purchased with His own blood" (Acts 20:28). How could the Apostle say that the blood shed was the blood of Christ if there were any duality in Christ in any sense? The same Apostle states in his first letter to the Corinthians: "For had they known it they would not have crucified the Lord of Glory" (2:8). The crucified one is the Lord of Glory Himself. There is no duality, and other passages state the same fact: "Great is the mystery of Godliness; God was manifested in the flesh" (Tim 3:16). "Who being in the form of God, counted it not a prize to be on equality with God, but emptied Himself, taking the form of a servant, being made in the likeness of men, and being found in fashion as a man, he humbled himself becoming obedient even unto death" (Phil. 2:6-8).

DANGER OF TWO NATURES

The expression "two natures united together" is theologically a dangerous one. It implies duality or even a kind of separation between the Godhead and the Manhood. Otherwise there would be no need to insist on the expression two natures - since there is a union. It does not denote a real union. Instead it expresses the existence of two separate natures coming together or combined together. Consequently, an expression like this lays one open to Nestorianism, condemned as a heresy by the Chalcedonian Churches. The expression "of two natures combined together" is a dangerous one in terms of our salvation. If there were two natures in Christ after the union, then the redemption of Christ was an act of His Humanity, for it is the flesh which was crucified. In which case the death of Christ would have no power to save the human race. The value of Christ's death lies in the fact that the one who was crucified was the Incarnate Word of God. Surely the Godhead did not suffer crucifixion, but the Godhead gave the crucifixion its infinite value and capacity to save all the human race. The expression "One nature which has the properties of the two natures", saves our belief in the redemption of our Lord. The expression "two natures" implies the possibility of a crucifixion of the flesh of Christ, but not of Christ Himself. All scriptural passages are against such an understanding. The blood, says St. Paul, is the blood of God: "The church of God, which He purchased with His own blood" (Acts 20:28).

RAPPROCHEMENT AND UNDERSTANDING

The subsequent history of Chalcedon with all its efforts aiming at a reconciliation between the Chalcedonians and the non-Chalcedonians has shown that rapprochement and a common understanding are possible if the problem is approached in the following spirit expressed by the twelfth century Armenian theologian and Catholicos Nerses IV:

Therefore, if One nature is said for the indissoluble and indivisible union and not for the confusion, and Two natures is said as being unconfused, immutable and indivisible, both are within the bounds of orthodoxy.

This statement was uttered by the Armenian Church leader in his continuous negotiations with the Byzantine Emperor, Manuel I Comnenus (1143-1180), for the reunion of the Armenian and Byzantine Churches. With this statement the Armenian Church is aware that there are different ways of expressing the same faith. Unity can be recovered and intercommunion restored beyond the words and formulae, if charity, good will and prayer become the driving force in the course of the negotiations. In the present negotiations the Armenian position has not changed. The Chalcedonian formula has of course come to stay. But the sense in which that formula was taken has fortunately gone. The council of Chalcedon had taken the words nature, person, and substance in their Nicaean sense and applied them to Christ, thus undoing by implication what Nicea had done. This was the real reason why the council incurred the stricture of the non-Chalcedonians. Through the centuries the Chalcedonians have done exactly the reverse by taking the word nature in a sense opposite to the one given in Nicaea. Therefore there is no reason to perpetuate the division created by the council of Chalcedon.

TWENTIETH CENTURY

For several years there have been regular meetings between the theologians belonging to the Chalcedonian and non-Chalcedonian churches. Meetings have been held in Aarhus (1964), Bristol (1967), Geneva (1970) and Addis Ababa (1971). The subject debated in the first two meetings was Christology. Does the Incarnate Christ have two natures or one, two wills or one? These conferences have made abundantly clear that, beneath variations of terminology, the Chalcedonian and non-Chalcedonian traditions share one and the same underlying faith. The content of the faith is the same for both, although the language in which that content is expressed may be different. The summary and conclusions issued by the Geneva consultation outlines the "Reaffirmation of Christological agreement", which reaffirms the results achieved at the two preceding meetings in Aarhus and Bristol:

We have affirmed our agreements at Aarhus and Bristol on the substance of our common Christology. On the essence of the Christological dogma our two traditions, despite fifteen centuries of separation, still find themselves in full and deep agreement with the universal tradition of the undivided church. It is the teaching of the blessed Cyril on the hypostatic union of the two natures of Christ that we both affirm, though we may use differing terminology to explain this teaching.

We both teach that Christ who is consubstantial with the Father according to the Godhead became consubstantial also with us according to humanity in the Incarnation, that He who was before all ages begotten from the Father, was in these last days for us and for our salvation born of the Virgin Mary, and that in Him the two natures are united in the one hypostasis of the Divine Logos, without confusion, without change, without division, without separation.

Jesus Christ is perfect God and perfect man, with all the properties and faculties that belong to Godhead and to Humanity. The human will and energy of Christ are neither absorbed nor suppressed by the divine will and energy nor are the former opposed to the latter, but are united together in perfect concord without division or confusion, he who wills and acts is always the one hypostasis of the Logos Incarnate. One is Emmanuel, God, and Our Lord and Saviour, whom we adore and worship.

However one cannot ignore the fact that the long period of separation has brought about certain differences in the formal expression of that tradition. The Chalcedonians accept seven ecumenical councils, the non-Chalcedonians only three. In the event of union, what status will the two sides assign to the fourth, fifth, sixth and seventh councils? Certain men are venerated as saints by one side, yet denounced as heretics by the other (Leo of Rome, Dioscorus of Alexandria, Severus of Antioch, etc). How are these anathemas to be lifted and the saints mutually recognised? How are the two sides to be integrated on the jurisdictional level? There are, for example, both Greek and Coptic Patriarchs in Alexandria, both a Chalcedonian and a Jacobite patriarch of Antioch. The Armenian Church has patriarchs in Jerusalem and Constantinople. How could they be related in the event of organic unity? The first two points concern the "localisation" of Holy tradition. The Byzantine Orthodox are committed to Chalcedon, the non-Chalcedonians are committed to the first three Ecumenical councils. The Geneva meeting suggested a possible escape from the impasse when they made the distinction between the "true intention of the dogmatic definition of the council" and the "particular terminology in which it is expressed, which the latter has less authority than the intention". The position of the Armenian theologians at the meetings was best expressed by Archbishop Tiran Nersoyan:

A Christian's loyalty is not to a council as such, but to the church as a whole, which itself is the highest Council, and which is the keeper of the deposit of the faith. The Council is judged by the faith of the Tradition and not vice versa. That is why some councils have been rejected by the Church ... others have been accepted universally or partially. ... Consequently, there is a hierarchy of Councils, both with respect to the importance ascribed to them and with respect to the extension of their reception. It is an historical fact that councils have been accepted after their statements have been the subject of further dialogue within the church.

Thus it might be possible for the non-Chalcedonians to accept the intentions of the fourth council as Orthodox, and to admit that what they rejected was primarily its formulation and terminology. The question of lifting of anathemas and the mutual recognition of saints was the main topic of the meeting held in Addis-Ababa (1971). In its official report the Addis Ababa consultation stated *"The lifting of anathemas ... seems to be an essential stage on the road to unity of the two traditions"*. The report continued, *"Once the anathemas pronounced against certain persons have been lifted it will not be necessary to require their recognition as saints by those who had so pronounced against them. Various national Churches have their calendars and lists of saints that differ. It is not necessary to impose uniformity in this matter"*. What would be necessary in case of lifting the anathemas would be for both parties to make an official declaration to the effect that there exists essential unity in faith between the two traditions, based on the doctrinal statement issued as a result of the consultations at Aarhus, Bristol and Geneva.

The question of traditions and jurisdiction in the national Churches, particularly the Armenian Church is not merely an administrative matter. In a church like the Armenian Church, religious and national identity are closely intertwined and its existence depends heavily on this factor. Having a substantial number of its members outside the geographical boundaries of the motherland, as a minority in the midst of other Christians the need of maintaining national jurisdictions and strengthening national traditions is fundamental. There is however room for variety, both in theological expressions and in canonical and liturgical practice.

The participants at the Addis Ababa consultation took the view that the time had come to move from the "unofficial level" to the "official level". In their report they conclude: "We hope that the work done at the unofficial level might be taken up officially by the churches." Towards the implementation of this hope the first steps have now been taken in order to turn this hope into reality. On the Chalcedonian side, the Inter-Orthodox Theological Commission for the dialogue with the non-Chalcedonian churches held its first meeting at Addis Ababa in 1971. Taking into account the work already done in previous meetings, the Commission affirmed that the two sides were now sufficiently prepared to embark on an official dialogue. The Commission went on to request the non-Chalcedonian churches to set up a corresponding commission, so that joint discussions could be arranged.

Later an unofficial consultation took place between the non-Chalcedonians and the Roman Catholics, similar in character to the conferences which the non-Chalcedonians and the Chalcedonian Orthodox churches have been having since 1964. In their joint declaration, the members of the conference spoke of their "Common foundation in the same apostolic tradition" as expressed by the first three Ecumenical Councils. "With one accord we reject alike the Nestorian and the Eutychian positions concerning Christ". They declared "We believe that our Lord Jesus Christ is God and Son Incarnate, perfect in his divinity and perfect in his humanity. His humanity is one with his divinity without confusion, without division, without change, without separation". Then they reaffirmed in general terms their differences in theological interpretation of the mystery of Christ which calls for further discussions.

It is clear that enough progress has been made to make a union between the Chalcedonian, non-Chalcedonian and the Roman Catholic churches possible and thus bring a valuable contribution in general to the ecumenical movement. It is hoped that all the leaders of the Churches would work hard for the realisation of the Church unity now that the groundwork has been done and basic differences resolved.

This study was first published in German translation in: Die Kirche Armenians. Eine Volkskirche Zwischen Ost und West. Hergb. Friedrich Heyer (Die Kirchen Der Welt Band XVIII). Evangelisches Verlagswerk Stuttgart, 1978.

FOR FURTHER READING

Arakel Aljalian, St Nerses Shnorhali, General Epistle. Translation and Introduction. St. Nerses Armenian Seminary, New York, 1996

Atiya, Asiz, Z. History of Eastern Christianity, University of Notre Dame Press, 1968

Frend, W.C. The Rise of the Monophysite movement: Chapters in the history of the Church in the fifth and sixth centuries, Cambridge University Press, 1972

Karekin Sarkissian. A brief introduction to Armenian Christian literature, 2nd printing, New Jersey, 1974

Kelly, J.N.D. Early Christian creeds, 2nd Edition, London, 1967

Vrej Nersessian, Das Beispiel Eines Heiligen: Leben und werk des Hl. Nerses Clajensis mit dem beinames Schnorhali, in Die Kirche Armeniens. Eine Volkskirche Zweschen Ost und West, Hersb. Friedrich Heyer. Evangelisches Verlagswerk, Stuttgart, 1978

Vrej Nersessian, Nerses IV Klayetsi, known as Shnorhali (full of grace), The Everyman Companion to East European Literature, edited by R. B. Pynsent & S. I. Kanikova. J. M. Dent, London, 1995

Nersoyan, Tiran, Archbishop, The Divine Liturgy of the Armenian Apostolic Orthodox Church With Variables, Complete Rubrics and Commentary. Revised Fifth Edition by Rev. Dr. Vrej Nerses Nersessian, SPCK, London, 1984

Nersoyan, Tiran, Archbishop, Armenian Church Historical Studies: Matters of Doctrine and Administration. Edited with an Introduction by Rev. Dr. Nerses Vrej Nersessian, St. Vartan Press, New York, 1996

ARMENIAN CHURCH DOCTRINE AND CHRISTOLOGY: STUDIES AND SOURCES

In the Christological controversies which embroiled Armenians and Greeks from the end of the fifth century onwards, catenae or collections of authoritative patristic quotations on the subjects in dispute, became one of the most useful weapons in the theologians' arsenal. Three Armenian sources of such doctrinal importance exist:

a) The correspondence between Eastern Patriarchs and Armenian Church leaders and theologians, contained in The Book of Letters (Tiflis, 1901) - a series of documents of primary importance for the understanding of the Armenian doctrinal position in Christology. It contains the Demonstration of Yovhannes Mandakuni among other documents. Translated partly into French and published with an introduction and notes by M. Tallon, S.J. *Livre des Lettres, les Groupe: Documents concernant les relations avec les Grecs*, in Melanges de l'Universite Saint Joseph, Liban, t. XXXII (1955).

b) *The Seal of Faith* (Ejmiacin, 1914) published by Karapet Ter-Mkrtchian. Recently re-published by Calouste Gulbenkian Foundation (Louvain, 1974). The book contains selections of doctrinal citations and treatise from existing works of the Church Fathers, attributed to Catholicos Komitas (610-628). See the article of Lebon, J., "Les citations patristiques du Sceau de la Foi, in Revue d'Histoire Ecclesiastique, t. XXV (1929).

c) The Root of Faith of Yovhannes Mayragomeci, compiled and completed in 1205. Thomson, R.W., The shorter recension of the Root of Faith, Revue des Etudes Armeniennes, n.s. V (1968).

Another important primary source published recently is The Teaching of Saint Gregory: An early Armenian catechism. Translation and commentary by R.W. Thomson (Harvard University Press: 1970, reprinted 2001). It contains an exposition of the Armenian position on the doctrine of the Trinity, and on the theology of the Incarnation, Redemption and Salvation.

On the first oecumenical councils in general, and on the council of Chalcedon in particular, see the collection of articles in Grillmeier and Bacht, Das Konzil von Chalkedon (1951-1954); Sellers, R.V., The council of Chalcedon: A historical and doctrinal survey (London, 1961); for its relation to Armenian Church consult Sarkissian, Garegin, The Council of Chalcedon and Armenian Church (London, 1965; reprinted New York, 1975); M. Ormanian, The Church of Armenia, Translated by M. Gregory,

2nd edition revised by Bishop T. Poladian (London, 1955). Timotheus Alurus' Widerlegung, ed. K. Ter-Mekertschian and E. Ter-Minassiantz, Leipzig, 1908. On the date of its translation see G. Ter-Minasyan, Patma-Banasirakan Hetazotoutyounner, Erevan, 1971, pp. 394-410.

For the articles submitted during the unofficial consultations between the theologians of the Eastern Orthodox and Oriental Orthodox Churches see The Greek Orthodox Theological Review, X, 2 (Winter 1964-1965); for the papers and minutes of the consultation between theologians of the Oriental Orthodox Churches and the Roman Catholic Church refer to Wort und Wahrheit, suppl. issue No- I (Vienna, 1971).

For a list of articles on the various aspects of the Armenian Church (History, doctrine, theology, worship, etc.) see Rev. Dr Vrej Nersessian, A Bibliography of articles on Armenian studies in Western journals 1869-1995 (Curzon in association with the British Library, London, 1997); Rev. Dr. Vrej Nersessian, Armenia (World Bibliographical Series volume 163), Oxford, 1993.

ABOUT THE AUTHOR

The Reverend Dr Vrej Nerses Nersessian was born in Tehran in 1948 and was educated at the Armenian College in Calcutta, the Gevorkian Theological Seminary in Holy Ejmiatsin, Armenia, and King's College London. He was formerly Head of the Christian Middle East section at the British Library (1975-2011). Among his many publications by the British Library is the recently published *Catalogue of the Armenian Manuscripts in the British Library acquired since the year 1913 and of collections in other libraries in the United Kingdom* (2012). He has contributed articles on the thought and culture of the Armenian Church in *The Blackwell Dictionary of Eastern Christianity*, ed. by Ken Parry (Blackwell, London 1999), *Jesus in History, Thought, and Culture, An Encyclopedia*, ed. by Leslie Houlden (ABC Clio, Oxford 2003) and *The Orthodox Christian World*, ed. by Augustine Casiday (Routledge, London 2012). He is married to Leyla Nersessian, has two sons Tiran and Zhirayr and two grandchildren: Levon and Anais.

Made in United States
Orlando, FL
13 July 2025